Published by:-
North Norfolk Railway plc
Sheringham Station
Sheringham
NR26 SRA
enquires@nnrailway.co.uk
www.nnrailway.co.uk
www.poppylineeducation.com

Copyright North Norfolk Railway plc 2012

Reprinted 2022 by Cheverton Printers of Cromer

ISBN 978-0-9571953-0-1

LOTTERY FUNDED

Quality Badge awarded by

Council for
Learning Outside the Classroom

CONTENTS

PAUL ATTERBURY

My introduction to railway carriage life came as a child, on the annual week in a British Railways camping coach. These were organised by my grandmother, who had taken her children on similar holidays in the 1930s. There were then hundreds of redundant carriages parked on remote sidings all over Britain, offering a kind of superior camping and great thrills to train-mad little boys like me. We usually went to Dorset, my introduction to the county where I now live. Basic cooking and comfort, paraffin lights, the ever changing roster of domestic duties, games in the evening, the carriage rocking in the night as trains roared past, shunting in the goods yard during the day, and wild games of cricket in the evenings when the locomotive had gone back to its shed, having our own keys to the station lavatories, the station master dropping in every morning to make sure everything was in order, all these are wonderful memories of those glorious weeks. It is no surprise, therefore, that I became interested in railway carriage houses, which of course were then very common. When I was much older I began to photograph the ones I found, and became absorbed by the history they could tell, and the way of life they represented.

Many years later, in 1987, and armed with a new determination to live in Dorset, I found by chance down a remote lane near the sea an old railway carriage sitting on its own in a large field. It was empty, and it did not take me long to track down the owners and persuade them to sell it to me. It was in a liveable condition, had electricity, one cold tap, even a telephone, an earth closet in a tumbledown shed that occasionally blew away, and was on a large site that had the makings of a great garden. Over the years my wife and I turned this old Great Western six wheeler of about 1903 into a comfortable home, while retaining the essential spirit of the carriage and its history. We lived there happily for many years and then moved on, tiring eventually of the constant maintenance and huge garden.

By now, railway carriage houses in original condition had become very rare and so I was very excited when I heard that the North Norfolk Railway planned to acquire and restore one, to ensure that future generations could appreciate the pleasures, and pitfalls, of railway carriage life. I was present when the completed carriage, fully restored and fully equipped, was formally opened, and it's huge appeal and educational value was immediately apparent. I could see that children would love it, offering as it did a window into a way of life quite beyond their experience or imagination. And so it has proved to be. I am delighted to have been a very small part of this project, and to have written this foreword to a book that will make the story of this, and similar railway carriage houses, accessible to a far wider audience.

3

INTRODUCTION

Railway carriage cottages and bungalows were once a common sight in many parts of our country, and they were important sources of homes for many people in the first half of the 20th century. As they have been replaced by new structures, or allowed to decay and disappear from our sight, so they have disappeared from our consciousness, taking with them a whole chapter of our social history that is now largely forgotten.

On many occasions the North Norfolk Railway Carriage and Wagon Department has been offered redundant coach bodies. These had either been used for spares or were renovated and put back on the rails to take pride of place in their fleet of vintage rolling stock. In 2008 the North Norfolk Railway had the idea of preserving a coach body as an example of social housing between the wars. This would be a unique resource that would become a fitting addition to our railway heritage. In 2009 the railway was offered a redundant coach body that had been used as part of a bungalow for 70 years. The North Norfolk Railway had the vision to see that this was an opportunity to restore the coach as a cottage, and so project 'Railway Cottage' was born.

left & right
Dr. Atterbury at
the opening
ceremony

The project was managed by the North Norfolk Railway's education department and was generously funded by the Heritage Lottery Fund. Planning permission was granted and the project got underway. The aim was to create a one carriage cottage, with a lean-to on the back, to look as it might have done in the mid 1930s. This was to involve researching information about carriage cottages in general and our carriage in particular, and finding appropriate furniture and artefacts of the period. A steering group was formed and the cottage came to life, both as a physical entity and as a database of information about such cottages and the way of life experienced by those who lived in them. The cottage was officially opened by Dr. Paul Atterbury on 30th April 2011.

Railway Cottage is unique both as an educational and museum resource and as a new creation of such a cottage in the 21st century. It stands as a testimony to the many thousands of people, who in times past, called such structures home and brings to light that once forgotten part of our history. Today the cottage is used as a learning resource; it is used by school children, provides opportunities for the public to visit and for reminiscences with the elderly. Hopefully it will continue to offer educational, historical and community opportunities well into the future.

COACH BODY HOMES

Redundant coach bodies were first used as homes in the late Victorian period. They were used primarily as holiday homes and were purchased by better off city dwellers who positioned them near to, or on the coast. The south and east coasts were especially popular with London dwellers as they could be easily reached using the railways. Dungeness beach in Kent was one of the early places subjected to this type of piecemeal development, where railway carriages were placed in a haphazard manner and then had huts and sheds built onto them to enhance the accommodation. Most were used as holiday homes, but a few were lived in by fishermen and their families as permanent homes.

Another place to experience early development using railway carriages was the beach at

Shoreham-by-Sea. This occurred after William Dickson, an American, established himself as one of the very first professional film makers there in April 1898. This predated the American film industry and the founding of Hollywood. The town of Shoreham was separated from the beach by the River Adur, and the film industry blossomed on the beach itself where a glass studio was built. In 1905 Mr. Lyndhurst bought the beach for £200.00 and the film industry enjoyed a rapid growth. As more and more people were employed by the industry so the requirement for accommodation became greater. In many cases actors and others built bungalow type accommodation on the beach above the high water mark. Many of these people found accommodation by buying redundant railway carriages from the nearby Lancing Railway Carriage Workshop for £10. They had them delivered by horse and lighter at low tide for £3 to the site of their choice as at this time there was no planning law against such development. The carriages were changed internally to make comfortable and acceptable accommodation with or without an external facade to make them look more like traditional bungalows. However there were no services, and even in the 1920s water had to be taken across the river in a large tank where it was sold for tuppence (2d) a bucket!

Although the film industry was over in Shoreham by 1910, the number of cottages and bungalows continued to grow, mainly as holiday homes. It became known as bungalow town and it is still an integral part of Shoreham to this day, with many of the bungalows still showing their railway carriage origins.

The 1920s & 1930s

The main period of railway carriages as homes, particularly permanent dwellings, was during the 1920s and 1930s. Soldiers returning from the Great War found that neither the promised jobs, nor housing were available. After the war, British farming returned to the recession it had been experiencing since 1870. Farmers were keen to sell off marginal and unproductive land and ex soldiers were able to secure a plot of land for £1. Many then purchased and put redundant railway carriages on their plots and used them as a basis for cottages and bungalows.

Victorian wooden coaches were being decommissioned as coach designs were changing. This was accelerated following the Quintinshill disaster of 1915. On the 22nd May of that year, following an error by a signalman, two trains collided head-on resulting in the deaths of 227 people with a further 246 injured. Contributory factors were wooden carriages that splintered, and gas lighting that set fire to the coaches. From that time railway companies looked to build coaches with metal skins and wooden coaches became redundant.

As the soldiers were demobbed they received any back pay owing to them and a small grant, which helped them to put a deposit down on a plot of land and purchase a redundant coach body. In Norfolk a redundant railway carriage could be purchased for £5 including delivery! This was just one option open to these ex-soldiers, and many others built shacks from whatever materials they could acquire, while others purchased and used redundant omnibuses or trams. These "plotlands" became established in many parts of the country where they formed communities practised in the art of sustainable living.

In North Norfolk there were plotlands, with railway carriage cottages, around Holt and High Kelling, Sheringwood and Aylmerton, mainly within wooded areas and served by tracks and roads. There were also a number of carriage cottages in and around Roughton, including the heath and the common.

> *Brian Gowing was brought up in Roughton in a single carriage cottage with his sister, that had what he described as a beach hut on the back for cooking. Initially there was no electricity, although they were eventually connected. Water had to be brought from a well using a yoke and two buckets. Cooking was done on an oil stove and later, after electricity was installed, a Baby Belling cooker. Brian can remember that the cottage was warm in the winter, although the wind could be heard howling underneath. His grandfather lived in a similar cottage on Roughton heath. When the family were finished with their carriages they set them on fire and were able to salvage five hundredweight of metal from the remains.*

In other parts of Norfolk there is still evidence of railway carriage cottages. There were some at Acle. Another report describes a carriage at the bottom of a garden near to a railway line just outside Norwich that appears on the deeds to the property in 1900 before the current house was built. A cottage made from 2 railway carriages, and still lived in, can be seen on the main road into Kings Lynn at South Wooton. This building is in excellent condition and the carriage features can still be seen on the outer walls. It is constructed in the classic tradition of such buildings with 2 carriages placed side by side with a gap between them, the ends blocked in with wood and a pitched roof put over both carriages.

There is a railway carriage cottage still in occupation situated close to the old Great Eastern Railway Station, at Aylsham, although it can no longer be recognised as such from the outside. Inside it still has some obvious features such as the ceiling curvatures that give away its origins. It is made from two coaches that were most probably built about 1890 and are thought to have been there since 1927. Other former coach body homes survive in a much dilapidated state at Edgefield and Banningham.

There are some carriage cottages still to be found on the coast, but these are now mainly holiday homes.

There were also a number of plotlands at Costessey where railway carriage cottages were constructed. Some of these were made from two carriages, but a number consisted of just a single carriage.

> *May Avon can remember moving to a two carriage cottage at Costessey with her family in 1925, when she was just three years old. Her father, who worked for the Midland and Great Northern Railway (M&GN) at Thorpe Station in Norwich, bought the two carriages and built the family cottage around them. One carriage housed two bedrooms and the other a small parlour and a larger living room that had a range where her mother did the cooking. Every Saturday night, after May and her sister had gone to their beds, her father made each of them a toffee walking stick which would be by their breakfast plate on Sunday morning. The central hallway was big enough to hold a piano and a walk in pantry. Outside there was a large shed with a copper for washing. Drinking water came from a well while other water needs were catered for by collecting rainwater in large water butts. Tragically May's father was killed in an accident at work and the family moved out of their carriage cottage in 1933*

One of the better known carriage cottages in North Norfolk was that belonging to William Marriott. Marriot was the Chief Engineer and Traffic Controller for the M & GN Railway between 1883 and 1924, when he retired. He was responsible for overseeing the railway line being extended from Melton Constable to Holt and Sheringham with Weybourne built as an afterthought in 1900.

After his retirement Marriott purchased two carriages and had them placed above the station at Sheringham on what is now Marriott's Way. They were positioned end to end and at ninety degrees to each other, forming an "L" shape. They were then converted to provide luxury holiday accommodation. Marriott and his family were able to enjoy many summer holidays in Sheringham overlooking the railway to which he had devoted so much of his working life.

During the 1920s and 1930s there were 3 railway carriages sited at Sheringham Station on what is now the main car park at the top of the town. At the time this area was part of the station yard. The carriages were used as accommodation for station staff. Occupiers included Mr. and Mrs. Cooper with their son Alfred, and Mr. and Mrs. Bill. George Cooper was a leading porter and Philip Bill was a clerk. Consequently there is a precedent for having Railway Cottage as part of the North Norfolk Railway.

RAILWAY COTTAGE—The Carriage

The carriage that forms the core of Railway Cottage was built by the Great Eastern Railway Company at their Stratford works in July 1899 to a design by their Locomotive Superintendent, Mr. James Holden. It was built as a second class five compartment carriage seating 60 passengers. It measures 27 feet in length and 9 feet in width. Special features of this carriage are the round topped doors. This was to prevent damage if a door was opened as it travelled as a commuter train through the Thames tunnel. It carried the number GER 524. Our carriage ran on the London suburban service out of London Liverpool Street Station, on the East London Line running to New Cross and Hither Green.

The service remained, and was operated by steam locomotives until 1962, when it was closed. They were hauled, initially, by engines such as the notorious 0-6-0 tank engines, known to their crew as "Buckjumpers" because of their spirited performance. Other engines included 2—4—2 tank engines nick named 'Gobblers' because of their coal consumption.

During its renovation the carriage gave up a few glimpses of its life when it was operational. A number of discarded bus tickets were found showing that people used the train after they have travelled to the station by bus just as commuters do today. These were issued by the London General Omnibus company and represent a number of routes. Most are for 1d fares, although one is for 1 1/2 d

and another is for a cheap day ticket using services 23 and 122. Others are for services 5 and 15. Tickets of those days had the route travelled by each bus printed on them. Tram tickets were also found advertising 'Drink Watney's Pale Ale' on the back.

Train tickets were found that had cost one penny (1d) and tuppence (2d). The tupenny ticket is highly appropriate as in 1874 the Great Eastern Railway's London terminus moved from Bishopsgate to the new terminus at Liverpool Street. Parliament granted permission for this move on condition that those members of the population who had been displaced and re-housed for the station development to take place would be provided with a train service so that they could continue their employment. Furthermore the conditions specified that the fare must not be more than tuppence for the return trip. By the year 1900 there were 23 "twopenny trains" terminating at Liverpool Street. Our carriage was clearly part of one of those trains at some time in its history.

Our coach was obviously a 'smoking coach', as seen etched into some of its windows and evidenced by empty packets of 'Woodbines' pushed down between the windows and doors.

Sweets for the journey included 'Riley's Toffees' given away by the wrappers found between the wooden flooring.

Also, found, discarded, was a ticket for a social and dance organised by the Women's Co-operative Guild, North Woolwich Branch. It was held in aid of the miners' relief fund in the Co-operative Hall, Kennard Street, North Woolwich on Monday 4th October 1926. It started at 7.30 p.m. and the Texas Band was in attendance. Entrance cost six pence (6d). On the back of the ticket was a dance card for gentlemen to book dances with the young lady who held the ticket. Sadly, this was empty. It is interesting to speculate whether the lady in question lost the ticket on her way to the dance or whether she dropped it on her return home. Did she return with her dreams unfulfilled or was she an ardent supporter of the general strike of that year and happy to support the cause? We will never know.

Our coach was re-numbered in 1923 as LNER 6631. It never carried passengers from that date and was retired from service in 1928.

13

'GLENHOLME'

After it was retired our carriage was sold to Mr. Jack Smith, who sited it, along with a sister carriage of the same design, at Kerdiston near Reepham. The carriages were placed side by side with a gap of six feet between them. A retired Victorian cattle wagon was placed across one end of the carriages (now part of the North Norfolk Railway goods vehicle collection). The gap was then filled in and a pitched roof constructed over the top of the wagon and carriages. The internal layout of the carriages was changed to create bedrooms and a lounge. The cattle wagon was extended on one side to make a cooking and living area. The whole structure became a carriage bungalow and given the name 'Glenholme'. The area of the surrounding land owned by Mr. Smith was about twenty acres.

Little is known about the bungalow's early years from 1930 to 1938, but in 1938 Jack Smith sold the property and land to Cecil Allen. He brought his young wife Edith (always known in the family as Betty), and his baby daughter Rhona, to live there. Cecil and Edith Allen were to live there for the rest of their lives. Cecil worked the land as a small holding and grew potatoes in sufficient quantities to sell. He also grew many types of fruit and vegetables for their own use. Edith kept chickens and sold the eggs. During the Second World War she sold them to airmen from the local airbase and later after the war they were purchased by the Egg Marketing Board. They kept a few pigs for meat and a Jersey cow for milk, and from the cream Edith churned their own butter. Cats and dogs were kept as pets and to keep vermin under control. Cecil also worked in the area as a jobbing builder.

Water came from a stream running close to the bungalow with a charcoal filter to purify the water. Initially there was an outside toilet and the "honey cart" came once a week! Later Cecil installed a bathroom and toilet in the carriage that now makes up Railway Cottage. Before such luxuries were available baths were taken in a tin bath and washing was done in a copper in an outside washhouse and shed.

A feature of the bungalow at this time was the parlour, which took up most of the Railway Cottage carriage. Edith would only allow people into this area on Sundays and special holidays, such as Christmas, and then it was generally only ladies!

Edith's niece, Jenny Bowers, can remember that her aunt Betty cooked on a small range and that she was a very good cook, producing a variety of tasty meals. Jenny used to go and stay at 'Glenholme' during some weekends when she would share a bedroom with her cousin Rhona. She would be collected from Reepham by her uncle Cecil. The girls found it easy to annoy her aunt Betty who would throw things at them. To escape they would rush into the bedroom and jump out of the window which they let down by its leather strap. Edith's sister, Joan Garrod, can remember that the family often met to have Christmas dinner at 'Glenholme'. It was held in the corridor between the two carriages. After dinner was over the ladies would do the washing up and then the men would retire to the kitchen where they played cards, while the women went to the parlour to talk. During the restoration of the carriage a Christmas cracker was found wedged down the side on a window. The joke reads:

"When is a soldier not a soldier?
Ans. When he is in quarters"

They both remember that peacocks and peahens turned up, although they do not know where from, and were encouraged to stay by Edith and Cecil. They bred there and soon there were many more!

Edith Allen was a keen gardener and took responsibility for the flower garden. This was extensive and a family photograph of the period, now in the possession of Mrs. Jenny Bowers, Edith's niece, shows both Edith and Cecil standing under an arch covered with a climbing rose. She also entered gardening competitions in Reepham with some success.

Earlier black and white photographs show Edith and Cecil separately on well manicured lawns. They look in the prime of life and so it must have been a tragic blow when they were predeceased by their daughter Rhona.

Cecil died some years before Edith. After his death she had milk and groceries delivered, and the postman remembers her well. Edith died in 1996. A report in the Eastern Daily Press records that her son-in-law sold the property in 1997 for £85,000.

The new owners, Mr. And Mrs. Jones added a brick extension to create a modern kitchen, dining and living area, as well as a porch. The bedrooms and bathroom were still in the carriages. Little else is known about their time at 'Glenholme' and they sold the property in 2002 to Richard and Serena Hilton.

Mr. and Mrs Hilton lived in the cottage with their young family until 2007, when they had a new house built on the land. Mr. Hilton has said that while it was fine to live in during the summer, the cottage could be very cold during the winter. They took the decision to donate one of the carriages to the North Norfolk Railway and it is due to their generosity that Railway Cottage has become a reality. The other carriage has become a playroom for their children.

RAILWAY COTTAGE - the construction

Carriage GER 524 began its final journey on 10th June 2010. It was lifted onto the back of a truck and carried from its location as part of 'Glenholme' to the North Norfolk Railway's station at Holt where it would become Railway Cottage.

The whole operation and journey went smoothly and it was lowered without incident onto its prepared foundation at Holt.

The next step was to prepare the foundation for the lean-to to be built on the back of the carriage which would form the main cooking and living area of the cottage. Originally, these were often little more than corrugated iron or wooden sheds with earth floors, providing a cheap extension to the property.

The lean-to for Railway Cottage was constructed from wood and had to conform, under planning regulations, to modern building standards, which included fire and health and safety regulations.

Most of the work was undertaken by Michael Biss and Jay Burton of Mid East Carpentry and Joinery. Between them they worked very hard through a summer of indifferent weather, and it was not long before the lean-to took shape.

Inside the lean-to the carriage had a door removed and a section of wall taken out to give complete access.

The brick chimney and fireplace were built for the range.

The 'topping out' was held on 10th September 2010 to celebrate the completion of the roof, which spans both carriage and lean-to.

Inside the cottage the carriage was divided into three compartments. The two end compartments became the adult bedroom and children's bedroom respectively. The central section became the parlour.

The lean-to is the main living and cooking area. In Railway Cottage the internal windows have been left as they were when it was a carriage and the etched 'smoking' signs are still visible.
In many cottages the internal windows were often painted over or blocked off with wood or cardboard to provide privacy.

Within the lean-to there is a sink but no running water. Some cottages used a well or pump within their plot, or the village pump or well There is also a pantry and a storage area for cleaning materials.

Outside the access ramps were built and the fence erected to define the grounds for the garden and outside sheds. It is likely that there would have been a wash house and accommodation for a pig, fed on household scraps and their manure then used on the garden.

Chickens were also an important part of the cottage economy and Railway Cottage has its own chicken run (without chickens, although a phantom chicken sometimes leaves an egg or two in the coop entrance!). Very few, if any, cottages had an inside toilet during the 1930s. Railway Cottage is no exception and there is an outside toilet within the garden area. It does not look inviting and does nothing to dispel the notion that such facilities were cold during the winter and smelly and fly ridden in the summer. Waste disposal was by means of a hole dug somewhere within the plot or by the weekly visit from the honeycart.

To make the cottage complete a garden was needed. All the accounts from people who lived in carriage cottages recall the gardens and the vegetables that were grown. In some cottages, for example 'Glenholme,' there was also a substantial flower garden.

Holt Station sits on one end of the Holt – Cromer ridge, a glacial moraine from the end of the last ice age. The site was once a gravel pit, extracting gravels that had been laid down as the ice retreated. Consequently the ground is hard packed gravel with large flints, typical of the area. The flower garden at the back of the cottage is planted in raised beds created with railway sleepers. The plants were all donated. The vegetable garden was made by using a JCB to dig out the area to a depth of about 30cm and filled with top soil.

It is planted up on a regular basis with seasonal vegetables. While not on the scale of original cottages it does give an idea of the way in which vegetables would have been grown to maximise the production of the garden and to provide food for the table in all seasons.

With the internal and external building work completed the cottage was ready to be furnished and turned into a 'home'.

RAILWAY COTTAGE - finishing touches

The decision was taken to make the cottage interior look the way a similar cottage might have looked in 1935. This meant accumulating the appropriate kitchen utensils, ornaments, furniture and other items that would have adorned such a dwelling. The larger pieces of furniture were bought from local antique shops and dealers and sourced from the internet. The education department was able to utilise some pieces that had been kept in store. An appeal was launched through the local free press and the response was wonderful. For some people it was an opportunity to pass on items and period artefacts that had been used by grandparents or other members of their family knowing that they would be appreciated for what they were. For others there was real nostalgia by donating items that reminded them of past relatives and seeing them set in the period from which they came.

The front door opens in to a hall complete with coats, hats.

The lean-to is furnished with an eclectic mix of wooden chairs and a kitchen table. One well used but comfortable arm chair is placed near to the range and the pipe on the mantel piece gives away that this is where the man of the house would sit. The sewing machine is testimony to the way in which many people of the period would make do and mend. This was much practised before the Second World

War, when it became a catch phrase as clothes were rationed. In the 1930s a skilful lady of the house would be able to make and mend her children's and husband's clothes.

A good set of scales are to be found with other useful food preparation equipment in the kitchen area together with some sturdy pans for the range. Those living there would have washed

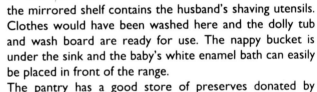

in the sink and the mirrored shelf contains the husband's shaving utensils. Clothes would have been washed here and the dolly tub and wash board are ready for use. The nappy bucket is under the sink and the baby's white enamel bath can easily be placed in front of the range.

The pantry has a good store of preserves donated by generous railway staff and volunteers and there is a meat safe to keep the flies off the food. Two rabbits hang ready for supper and a mouse trap keeps the vermin at bay.

Opposite the pantry is where the cleaning utensils are kept. There is a carpet beater and scrubbing brushes and shoe cleaning equipment. Also kept here is a cobbler's last, hammer and tacks for essential boot repairs.

In front of the range there is a rag rug. This was made especially for Railway Cottage. In the centre of the rug is the "eye of the house" which protects the cottage from all evil!

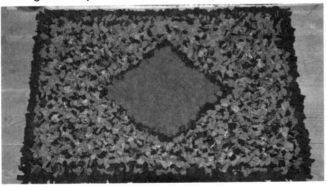

On the mantel piece are two matching examples of trench art from the First World War. Such items became common during and after the war as they were made by many soldiers in the trenches, who used the abundant shell cases to fashion decorative items.

On the shelves to the left of the range is a tea set. This donated set was originally obtained during the 1930s by collecting coupons from tea packets. It is still complete with its tea pot, milk and sugar bowl as well as cups, saucers and plates. The transfer printed pattern is still fresh and colourful.

In the parlour there are two china dogs on the top shelf of the shelf unit. These dogs originally belonged to Edith Allen when this coach was part of 'Glenholme' and they were kept in this carriage. They are the only original artefacts in the cottage from that time and were generously donated by Edith's sister Mrs.

Joan Garrod, who had kept them since Edith's death.

Also in the parlour on top of the bureau and below a hand coloured photograph of a Grenadier Guardsman is a small box. This contains First World War medals and other memorabilia from the war.

The adults' bedroom has the double bed pushed against one of the walls. Period photographs of carriage cottages mainly show beds pushed into corners in this manner. The bed was purchased with funds from the National Lottery grant, while the wonderful patchwork bed spread was made locally especially for the cottage, just as were the two quilts on the beds in the children's room. There are chamber pots under all the beds - essential items in such dwellings to avoid a trip to the outside toilet on a cold or wet night!

On the dressing table are a lady's hairbrush and vanity mirror, as well as hairbrushes for a gentleman. These have all been donated. Opening drawers and the wardrobe will reveal clothes of the period including garments hand knitted by local ladies to 1930s' patterns.

The beds in the children's bedroom were purchased using the National Lottery Grant and are typical of children's beds of the period. There is a model castle and farm that have been made for the cottage by a member of the Poppyline Education Group to a 1930s' pattern. The lead soldiers on the castle have also been handmade and painted. It would have been lucky children indeed that would have had such a talented father who could make such toys. They would probably have been made in secret for Christmas with excited children awakening on Christmas morning to see what Father Christmas had brought them — if they had been good!

The garden was stocked with plants that were generously donated by a variety of members of the local community. It was not possible in the space available to recreate the smallholdings which would have been worked by folk that lived in coach body homes but there are vegetables, herbs and fruit. The outside area became an extension of the living space for washing and drying clothes, beating carpets, doing repairs and chopping wood. Food would have

been grown in every available place to make sure that there was always a good supply to feed the family all year round. Railway Cottage garden is maintained by members of the Poppyline Education Group.

Railway Cottage is well furnished and equipped with the everyday items of the period. This would have been quite normal for such a cottage. Living in a railway carriage should not be equated with living in poverty. Certainly there were down sides, but there were many brick and mortar houses in this country during the 1920s and 1930s that had outside toilets and wash houses and where the conditions were cramped and considerably worse than those to be found in a railway carriage cottage. Most men who lived in plotlands and cottages worked and brought in an income, as well as running their own small holding. It is likely that most of these coach body homes and small holdings were owned by the occupants, and much pride was taken in improving them and making them comfortable. It could be argued that they were preferable to tied or rented housing which was the only option for most

working class families. Some relatives remember the sadness when they moved away from their coach body home and recall their lives there with fondness and nostalgia. It is hoped that Railway Cottage reflects this care and affection.

BILLY GALLANT

Railway Cottage is used as an integral part of the North Norfolk Railway's education programme providing living history activities for school children and reminiscence opportunities for others. All visitors are encouraged to handle many of the objects and artefacts; this is a unique experience as many visitor attractions discourage or prohibit touching and handling. To help to bring it to life for school children and others, a fictitious family have been invented to live in the cottage—Mr. and Mrs. Billy Gallant. Although William Gallant was a real person in history the following biography is fictitious.

William Albert Thomas Gallant was born in 1894 and had an upbringing typical of so many people living in the country at that time. In 1908 at the age of 14 years he started to work for the Midland and Great Northern Railway and stayed with them until 1914 when he joined the Norfolk Regiment and fought with them in the Great War until it ended in 1918. He was wounded once when he was hit by shrapnel in his left leg. This piece of shrapnel can be found in the box containing Billy's memorabilia on top of the bureau. He survived the war.

After being demobbed Billy rejoined the Midland and Great Northern Railway as a platelayer, working between Holt and Weybourne. A platelayer is responsible for inspecting and maintaining the track by greasing points and watching for wear and tear. He was one of the lucky ones who did come back to a job! Shortly afterwards he married Florence, known as Flo in the family. Flo's brother was killed in the Great War and his photograph hangs above the bureau in the parlour, dressed in his uniform of the Grenadier guards. Billy moved into the coach body and together he and Flo created a happy and comfortable home. Billy and Flo had three children. The eldest, Margaret, was born in 1927 with son Thomas following in 1930. The youngest child was Rose who was born in 1935. Visitors to the cottage can imagine Flo cooking on the range, while the accoutrements of a well lived in dwelling are all around and Billy's boots are by the fire.

Such a background gives children a perspective not only of what life would have been like at that time, but also the depth of history and experience through which a person of the era would have lived. The cottage is not just a one dimensional exhibit, but a three dimensional witness to history.

RAILWAY COTTAGE - now and the future

Railway Cottage is used in a number of ways. With primary school children it plays an important role in providing experience of what domestic life may have been like for evacuees on the home front during the Second World War. Children arrive in appropriate costume and take on the roles of evacuees, starting with a steam train ride from Sheringham to Holt. At Holt they undertake a number of workshops that involve them role playing similar experiences to those of real evacuees during 1940. The boys dig for victory in the cottage garden while the girls help with household chores including cleaning, bed making and washing. Billy Gallant's biography is brought up to date by having him join the Home Guard.

Railway Cottage puts the children in a period setting and so enhances the atmosphere and allows them to empathise with their counterparts of 1940. This is an inspired way of teaching history by taking pupils out of the classroom and using their natural ability to role play using their imagination.

The cottage is used for reminiscence sessions. These involve the use of artefacts, discussion and music to help people to remember their younger days. The cottage provides a perfect atmosphere that acts as a stimulus for participants. As the years move on so the main groups using this facility will come from those born during the 1940s, then the 1950s followed by the 1960s and so on. It is remarkable how little some every day household items changed during the period from the 1930s to the 1960s! There were still a considerable number of railway carriage cottage in use as permanent residences during that time.

Railway Cottage is open to the public at weekends when steam trains are running. This gives people an opportunity to appreciate the cottage and to discuss it and its contents with well informed volunteers. It is a cross generational experience as grandparents and grand children explore the cottage together.

The development of Railway Cottage has been a project that has brought together many organisations as well as the local community and individuals who have worked as a team to bring to life a little piece of our recent history. It has been successful as a project of co-operation as well as a stunning testimony to the people who lived In such dwellings and called them home. People lived in them, children were born and grew up, they played, some were married from them, people laughed and cried, celebrated, knew happiness and sorrow and in some cases died in them. Hopefully, Railway Cottage will continue to provide a living example of that part of our social history lost in the early 20th century, where the resilience of people provided for themselves (when governments and policy let them down) well into the future,.

The last word is given to some of those people who have visited Railway Cottage:

'A lovely exhibit—interesting and rare to be able to touch. Thank you.'
Louise Everitt; Ipswich

'A great journey back in time'
A. Gulligan, Aberdare

'A fascinating reminder of our past and an eye opener for the grandchildren. Good luck with the venture'
Norma King

ACKNOWLEDGEMENTS

The author wishes to thank all those who provided generous help, support and advice during the writing and production of this book.

The North Norfolk Railway plc Education Department has undertaken the publication of this book. Dr. Paul Atterbury has not only written the foreword, but also commented on the text, offered invaluable advice and provided materials. Simon Miller undertook the research on our coach body and has generously allowed this to be used. Andy Phillips had given advice on some of the historical aspects of coach bodies. Dave King of the Marriott Museum has made available documents and archive of the Midland and Great Northern Railway. Mrs. Jenny Bowers, niece of Edith Allen, and Mrs. Joan Garrod, sister of Edith Allen provided many memories of life in 'Glenholme'. Mrs. May Avon told us her vivid memories of living in a railway carriage cottage as a child, as did Brian Gowing who lived in a single coach cottage at Roughton. Alan Childs kindly commented on the text. Lesley Carrick has proof read each update of the text. The printing of this book has only been possible with generous funding from the Heritage Lottery fund. Last, but by no means least, thanks to Jenny Phillips who spent many hours working on the layout of this book, as well as tracking down permission to use some materials.

Thanks are expressed to all those who have given permission to use photographs. Copyright remains with the photographers or owners of the images. Alistair McDougal, Nigel Scarlett, William Marriott Museum, Alan Childs, Andy Phillips, Jenny Bowers, Ron Weibe, Chris Shore for the Dungeness photographs, Fitzhouse Books, London Transport Museum and George Carrick. The Shoreham-by-Sea photos are supplied by kind permission of the family of Doris Steers, late of Shoreham-by-Sea, West Sussex. Thanks also to the children from North Walsham Junior School.

Thanks are given to the following who gave their support to the Railway Cottage project. Serena and Richard Hilton, The Museums, Library and Archives Council, Midland and Great Northern Joint Railway Society, John Smith, Chris Green, Bob Wright, Mid-East Carpentry and Joinery, local traders, 36 patch workers, 18 knitters, Cathy McNally who made the rag rug, all those who donated over 300 items and artefacts and all the members of the Poppyline Education Group who gave freely of their time and energy to ensure that this project became the success that it is.